for BEGINNERS

Geoff Carless

Adam & Charles Black
London

The publishers and author wish to thank the following for their assistance with the production of this book: Belstaff International Limited, Stoke-on-Trent; Griffin Helmets Limited, Halesowen; Kawasaki Centre, Northampton; R. Saluz, Poole; The Department of the Environment.

Published by A & C Black (Publishers) Ltd
35 Bedford Row
London
WC1R 4JH

ISBN 0 7136 2597 X

This book is copyright under the Berne Convention. All rights are reserved. Apart from any fair dealing for the purpose of private study, research, criticism or review, as permitted under the Copyright Act, 1956, no part of this publication may be reproduced, stored in a retrieval system, or transmitted in any form or by any means, electronic, electrical, chemical, mechanical, optical, photocopying, recording or otherwise, without the prior permission of the copyright owner. Enquiries should be addressed to the Publishers.

Copyright © Geoff Carless, 1979, 1980, 1984

Reprinted 1980, 1984

Photography by Geoff Carless
Design by Brian Wilkins

Printed in Great Britain by Hollen Street Press Ltd, Slough

Contents

The Author 4
Introduction 4

Part One
The Motorcycle and Protective Clothing 5
Buying your first motorcycle 5
Borrowing a motorcycle 6
The First Ride 6
Training schemes 6
The controls 7
Starting and stopping engines 10
Two-stroke and four-stroke engines 12
The choke 12
Daily and weekly checks 13
The clutch 14
The gearbox 15
Clothing 16

Part Two
The Law 19
Basic Requirements 19
Maintenance Requirements 21

Part Three
On the Road 22
Riding position 22
Operation of controls 23
Changing gear 24
Stopping 25
Riding drill 27
Manoeuvring 27
Arm signals 28
Turning left 29
Turning right 30
Crossroads 31
Entering main roads 33
Roundabouts 34
Dual carriageways 36
Gradients 38
Pedestrian crossings 39
Overtaking 41
Night riding 43
Adverse conditions 44
Observation 45
Parking 46
Motorways 47

Part Four
Taking the Test 49
The test 49
Hints on taking your test 49
The Highway Code 50
Do's and don'ts 52
Road signs 54

The Author

Geoff Carless was born in Solihull in 1949 and developed an interest in motorcycles almost from that date. Both his father and grandfather owned motorcycle combinations, and sitting in the sidecar was his main means of travel.

Before leaving school Geoff passed the Cycling Proficiency Test, after deciding that road safety was a very important factor in staying alive. He bought his first motorcycle as soon as he was old enough to have a licence and has rarely been without one ever since.

In 1971 Geoff Carless joined the Police with the sole ambition of becoming a Traffic Patrol Motorcyclist. After passing both the Advanced Motorcycle and Advanced Car Driving courses to Grade 1 standard he joined the Traffic Department, serving two years on the bikes and one year on Motorway Patrol duty.

In 1977 Geoff Carless became a Motorcycle Journalist, joining the staff of *Motorcycling*.

Publisher's Note
The photographs in this book show a 250cc motorcycle. As from 1 February 1983, learners are restricted to machines with a maximum capacity of 125cc.

Introduction

Today's road and traffic conditions can be lethal, even for the most experienced rider, so it is important that everyone who intends to ride a motorcycle has some form of training or instruction.

It seems to be the case that when some car drivers see a learner rider, or a moped rider, they are overcome by an uncontrollable urge to overtake him. Whether it is just another challenge, or whether the car driver feels safer with the bike behind him, is not really known, but it does happen. Cars pull out of sideroads into the path of motorcycles, causing some horrific injuries for the rider. These are reasons why new riders need to learn defensive riding. I always ride with one thought in mind, 'Treat everyone else with great care and you won't go far wrong.'

This book will give you an insight into defensive riding, with the emphasis on preparing for, and taking, your test, but it must be accompanied by plenty of practice. Theory is not enough; only practice makes perfect.

GEOFF CARLESS

PART ONE
The Motorcycle & Protective Clothing

Section One

Buying Your First Motorcycle

Choose a machine that is standard in its riding position because a bike that has been altered to look like a racing bike will probably be uncomfortable to ride, and may be very difficult to balance at low speeds.

There are very few problems when buying a new machine as you will have the guidance of a salesman and the backing of a warranty. Buying secondhand is a different story, and extra care should be taken. Ask a friend who is knowledgeable about motorcycles to have a look at any bikes you like, or that are in your price range. He should ride the bike and give you his impressions. Ideally, you should ask a mechanic to listen to the engine for you – noises give a lot away about the condition of the engine.

If you are totally new to motorcycling, and do not know anyone else with a bike, go along to your local motorcycle club. You will almost certainly find someone there willing to help.

Borrowing a Motorcycle

If you are able to borrow a moped or motorcycle it may save you a lot of money, especially if you intend to buy a bigger bike after passing your test. The main point to remember concerns insurance. You must either insure it yourself, or have your name added to the owner's insurance policy. Think it over carefully because if you are involved in an accident whilst on someone else's policy they could lose their no-claims bonus which will be expensive.

It is in the owner's interest that you keep his machine, and yourself, completely within the law. Most offences concerning the bike's documents and road tax, and a few offences connected with its use on the road are the responsibility of the owner and the rider.

The First Ride

A lot of accidents occur within the first few miles of a basic beginner collecting his first motorcycle from a shop. Never use the roads to experiment. You have to learn balance, clutch control, braking, manoeuvring, acceleration and much, much more. If you cannot arrange for your new bike to be collected yourself ask the dealer to deliver it for you.

Find a quiet piece of land, a disused car park, or somewhere similar in order to get used to the bike before you venture onto the roads. If there is a STEP or RAC/ACU training scheme operating in your area take advantage of it, you will receive individual and expert tuition.

Remember, the greater the time you spend getting used to your bike, learning its controls and characteristics, the better you will be as a rider on our roads.

Training Schemes

Wherever possible you should take advantage of the training offered by one of the schemes operated in your area. Both the STEP and RAC/ACU training schemes are being held within easy reach of almost everybody. There is a small charge for their services, but when buying a new motorcycle, and sometimes a secondhand machine, the dealer will often offer to pay the fee as an incentive.

Many dealers will also offer to deliver your new motorcycle to the scheme of the your choice so that you can be given expert tuition off the road, before having the worry and danger of that first trip on the roads.

Details of the schemes operating in your particular area can be obtained from your local dealers and motorcycle clubs.

Section Two

The Controls

Automatic Mopeds

Brakes
The brakes on an automatic moped are similar in position and operation to those of a bicycle. The lever on the lefthand side of the handlebars works the back brake, and the righthand lever works the front brake.

Throttle
The righthand side of the handlebars has a twistgrip which is turned to increase or decrease engine speed, thus making the bike go faster or slower.

Decompression Lever
Found on the handlebars, usually the left side, this lever is used to reduce the effort required for starting the engine.

Starter Clutch
Yet another lever on the handlebars. It is used to connect the pedals to the engine for starting.

Choke
Found in various positions (consult your bike's handbook), it is used for supplying a richer mixture to the engine for cold starting.

Disconnection Mechanism
Found in various positions and used for disconnecting the engine so that the bike can be pedalled along.

Fuel Tap
Found near the fuel tank. It has three positions: On, Off and Reserve. It should be turned 'off' when not in use, and set to 'on' for normal riding. The reserve position allows you to get to a petrol station when the fuel runs out in the 'on' position.

Electrical System
This usually only operates when the engine is running.

Centre Stand
Used to hold the bike upright when parked. It is only designed to take the weight of the machine so do not abuse it.

New Type Auto Mopeds
(After August 1977)
These mopeds have footrests and a kickstart, together with a rear footbrake instead of a handlebar lever. Machines do vary so consult the handbook for the location of the controls.

Motorcycles

Front Brake
A lever located on the righthand side of the handlebars.

Rear Brake
Foot operated pedal located by the righthand footrest (on some Italian machines and older British ones it is found on the lefthand side).

Throttle
Twistgrip on the righthand side of the handlebars, used for increasing and decreasing engine speed.

Gear Lever
Foot operated pedal located by the

lefthand footrest (on some Italian machines and older British ones it is found on the righthand side).

Clutch

Lever located on the lefthand side of the handlebars. It is used for connecting and disconnecting the engine to the rear wheel.

Starter

The majority of machines up to 250cc have a kickstart lever, normally located on the righthand side of the engine, but some bikes are now fitted with electric starter motors, similar to those on cars. The starter button is usually found on the righthand side of the handlebars near the throttle.

Electrical Switches

The two handlebar switch clusters contain the following: indicators, dip-switch, horn, engine cut-out and lights. Warning lights for main-beam, oil and neutral are also provided.

Oil Filler Cap

The oil in a four-stroke engine should be checked during regular maintenance, but that in a two-stroke should be checked each time the bike is refuelled. Most two-strokes now have a separate lubrication system with the oil contained in a tank located by the seat, although the mix-in-the-tank type two-strokes are still available.

Fuel Tap

Found near the fuel tank, it has three positions: on, off and reserve. It should be turned 'off' when not in use, and set to 'on' under normal running conditions. The reserve position allows enough fuel in the tank to get you to a filling station when the 'on' position runs out.

Some bikes are fitted with diaphragm-type taps. They have three positions: on, reserve and prime. The 'on' position is used for normal running, and can be left on all the time because fuel will only flow when the engine is running. The 'prime' position is used to by-pass the diaphragm operation and thus aid starting when the 'on' positions runs out. After starting the engine on 'prime' the tap should be turned to the 'reserve' position.

Sports Type Mopeds

A lot of smaller bikes which look like motorcycles are in fact mopeds. The pedals can be locked into footrest positions for easier riding.

Starting and Stopping Engines

Starting Auto Mopeds

1. Stand on the lefthand side of the machine with it on its centre stand.
2. Switch the fuel tap to 'on'.
3. Operate the choke if starting from cold (on some bikes the carburetter will have to be primed – see owner's handbook).
4. Turn the pedals until the left one is just forward of its top central point.
5. Hold the front brake on and keep your weight forward so that the rear wheel is clear of the ground.
6. Open the throttle slightly.
7. Pull up the decompression lever.
8. Kick the pedal down sharply and release the lever just before the pedal reaches the bottom of its stroke.
   If the engine only has a starter clutch the lever should be held in until the engine fires.
9. Allow the engine to warm up and then push in the choke lever.
10. The throttle can be closed when the engine is running and the rear brake applied to stop the rear wheel spinning.

Stopping Auto Moped Engines

Bikes with a decompressor are stopped by closing the throttle and operating the decompressor lever. Those not fitted with a decompressor are stopped by using the electric cut-out button on the handlebars after first closing the throttle.

Never rev an auto moped with the brakes on. You will burn out the clutch.

Starting New Type Mopeds (Those fitted with kickstarts)

1. Stand on the righthand side of the bike with it on its centre stand.
2. Switch the fuel tap to 'on', and use the choke if necessary.
3. Turn on the ignition.
4. Hold the front brake on with your weight forward to keep the rear wheel clear of the ground.
5. Place your instep on the kickstart and open the throttle slightly.
6. Kick down sharply.
7. Let the engine warm up, and return the choke if necessary.
8. When the engine is ticking over, the throttle can be closed and the rear brake applied to stop the rear wheel spinning.
9. The bike can now be pushed off the stand for riding.

Stopping New Type Moped Engines

This is done by operating the decompression lever or engine cut-out button after first closing the throttle. Do not forget to switch off the ignition.

Starting Motorcycles

1. Sit astride the machine with it off its stand.
2. Ensure that the gearbox is in neutral – do not rely on the neutral indicator light, but roll the bike slightly backwards and forwards to check.
3. The fuel tap should be switched to the 'on' position and the choke operated if necessary.
4. Switch on the ignition and open the throttle slightly.
5. Kick down the kickstart lever, or operate the electric start button, until the engine fires.
6. Allow the engine to warm up on a fast tickover before closing the choke, if it has been used.

The kickstart lever, usually found on the righthand side, can be turned out of the way when not in use.

Stopping Motorcycle Engines

With the throttle closed you can either switch off the ignition or operate the engine cut-out button. Remember to turn the fuel tap to 'off' if the bike is not going to be used for some time.

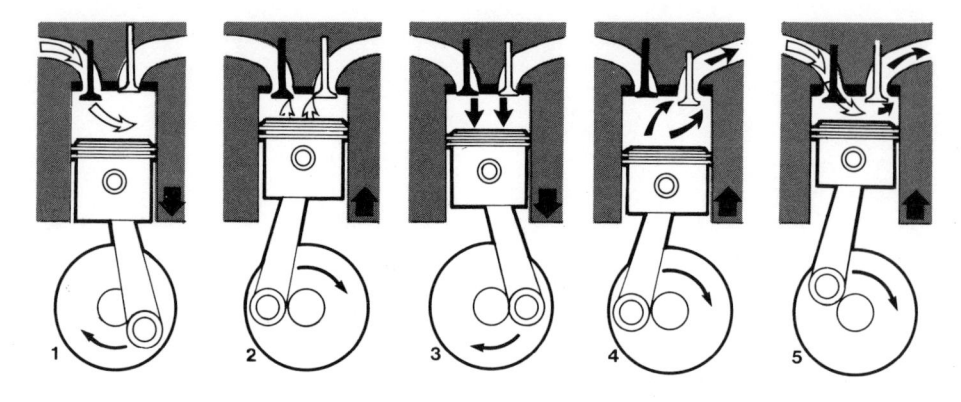

4-Stroke Engine
1. As the piston descends it creates a vacuum and draws in the fuel/air mix through the inlet valve;
2. As the piston starts to rise both the valves are closed causing the mixture to be compressed;
3. The spark plug ignites the mixture and the force from the explosion pushes the piston down;
4. As the piston comes up on stroke three, the exhaust valve is open allowing the burnt gases to be pushed out;
5. The cycle starts again using the exhaust valve for a fraction of a second to help draw in the mixture;
6. The valves are controlled by a camshaft.

2-Stroke Engine
1. As the piston rises it compresses mixture in the chamber, and draws more mixture into the partial vacuum in the crankcases. The piston itself operates the inlet and exhaust ports;
2. At around top dead centre the spark plug ignites the mixture and the explosion forces the piston down, at the same time compressing the mixture in the crankcases;
3. Just after the piston passes the exhaust port it opens other ports which allow the fresh mixture under pressure to find its way from the crankcases to the compression chamber, and the cycle starts again.

Two-Stroke and Four-Stroke Engines

Now that most two-stroke motorcycles have separate lubrication systems and no longer require the owner to mix the petrol and oil in the tank, the choice of which to buy is purely a personal one. Four-stroke engines are becoming more popular, because of the exhaust emission regulations. They are easier to service, more economical, and less prone to fouled plugs.

Two-strokes are still available but will slowly be phased out completely.

On the road the only noticeable difference between the two is that the four-stroke offers greater engine braking than the two-stroke.

The Choke

In simple terms the choke is a mechanical device which, when operated, alters the fuel/air mix in the carburettor. It increases the amount of petrol to allow easier starting when the engine is cold.

Always check that the choke is fully closed when the engine is running at its normal temperature. Leaving it partially open can result in rough running or even lead to the engine cutting out altogether.

Consult your handbook to locate the choke on your bike. It may be a lever on the carburetter or a car type button and cable on the handlebars. Make sure you know which way is 'on' and which way is 'off'.

Daily Checks

1. Petrol – have you got enough for your journey?
2. Oil level – engine and two-stroke.
3. Lights – including brake light and indicators.
4. Horn.
5. Rear suspension units – adjust to a stiffer setting if you are carrying a pillion passenger
6. Cleanliness of lights and number plate
7. Running brake test – traffic conditions permitting, test the brakes from about 10–15mph to ensure correct operation

Weekly Checks

1. Tyre pressures
2. Clutch adjustment
3. Brakes adjustment
4. Rear drive chain tension
5. Battery electrolyte level
6. Wheel spokes – check for loose ones
7. Check all nuts and bolts for security.
8. Lubricate rear drive chain

All the above checks are usually found in the owner's handbook that accompanies the bike.

Section Three

The Clutch

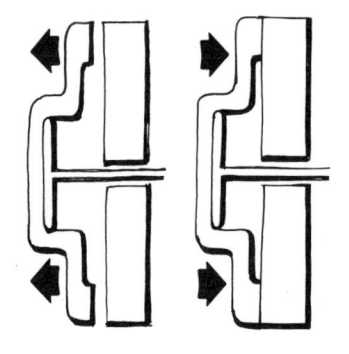

Basic clutch operations:
1. Clutch operated, plates separate;
2. Clutch released, drive engaged again.

The purpose of the clutch is to connect and disconnect the power of the engine, via the gearbox, to the backwheel. On small machines they vary in that they can have one or more clutch plates, whereas larger machines have multi-plate clutches. The plates being the actual surfaces that come into contact when the clutch is operated.

To separate the plates and disengage the clutch the handlebar lever is pulled in towards the rider. It therefore follows that if the lever is not pulled in, but remains in its 'normal' position, the clutch plates are engaged.

Starting the Engine

Normally, when starting the engine using a kickstart or an electric starter, the clutch lever is not touched. On some machines, however, the clutch has to be pulled in to activate a safety device which prevents the bike lurching forward if it is in gear, before the electric starter will operate.

General Operation

The clutch is used for moving away from a standstill, stopping and changing gear. Its correct use for each is explained on pages 23 and 25.

Automatic Mopeds

Automatic mopeds with only one gear have permanently engaged clutches, and no lever to worry about. When the throttle is opened the bike will move.

Revving the engine with the brakes on will result in a burnt out clutch. Treat the clutch carefully.

Section Four

The Gearbox

If you think back to your cycling days you will appreciate how much easier it is to ride a bike with gears. By selecting the appropriate gear it is possible to maintain the same speed with less effort, or increase the speed with the same effort. The same principle applies to the motorcycle, but this time the engine does the work, not your legs.

Modern motorcycles up to 250cc have either 5 or 6 speed gearboxes, but their method of operation is the same. As the gear pedal is lifted or depressed the selectors move the drive to the next gear. When the pedal is released it returns to its ready position and awaits the next selection. Unlike a car, the motorcycle gearbox cannot be used to jump gears; for example from 4th to 1st or 5th to 3rd. The intermediate ratios have to be used; changing up you have to change 1st to 2nd, 2nd to 3rd, 3rd to 4th, and so on. Changing down it has to be 5th to 4th, 4th to 3rd, 3rd to 2nd, 2nd to 1st.

As speed increases it becomes necessary to select a higher gear, but at what point should you actually select the next ratio?

If your bike is fitted with a rev counter alongside the speedometer it will indicate engine speed. A red line – or sector – is shown as the safe maximum rpm for the engine, but it is **not** a good idea to use this line for gear changes. Apart from putting undue stress on the engine, it is usually past the actual point of maximum power. Familiarity with your own machine and your own style of riding will tell you the best rev counter reading to change gear for normal riding, and the best point for high speed riding.

If you do not have a rev counter you will have to rely on the feel of the engine. There is a point where acceleration will tail off quite noticeably. You can also use the speeds recommended in the owner's handbook for guidance.

Automatics

In the smaller classes of machines those referred to as automatics usually have a single speed with an automatic clutch. They do not have automatic gearboxes as their name suggests.

The gear pedal can be turned on its locating splines so that it is near to your foot when riding

15

Section Five

Clothing

Having bought your new, or secondhand, motorcycle, you will now need safe and adequate clothing, and it is important that you allow enough money in your budget to buy all you will need.

Comfort is an important safety factor when riding a motorcycle. It is no fun wearing an old anorak and jeans when it is pouring with rain. The water runs down your neck, the jeans stick to your legs and you become dangerously uncomfortable. You concentrate on your discomfort rather than your riding. Buy the best you can possibly afford – it pays in the long run.

Be safety conscious when buying your clothing. Buy bright coloured clothing, or, if you do decide to buy black, wear a reflective bib or belt.

Helmet

Apart from being required by law, the crash helmet is probably the single most important item. There are many makes and designs on the market, but they all fall into one of two categories, open face (jet style) or full face.

The full face helmet offers greater protection to the face, because it has a chin bar, but care should be taken to buy one that has a large aperture for good vision. The visor is clipped to the outside of the helmet and can be raised or lowered as required.

The open face helmet does not offer facial protection, but does allow the choice between a visor, goggles or peak and visorette. They are more popular with the riders of mopeds and very small motorcycles.

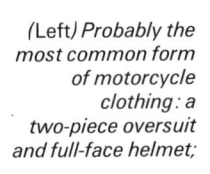

(Left) Probably the most common form of motorcycle clothing: a two-piece oversuit and full-face helmet;

(Right) The alternatives: a one-piece oversuit and open-face helmet, worn by many moped and very small bike riders.

Visors and Goggles

The visors available for full face helmets are designed for individual models and are not always interchangeable. They vary between thin standard visors and the Griffin 2.5mm Heatshields used by Grand Prix racing drivers. Heated visors are also available, working on the same principle as the heated rear window in a car.

After a while a visor will become scratched and therefore useless. Whilst it may seem okay in fine weather and daylight, it will cause starring and poor vision in rain and low light. Renew it and keep your vision clear.

Tinted visors are also available, although institutes like the Optical Information Council deplore their use and recommend a standard visor with either sunglasses, or an extra clip-on tinted strip that can be removed in an emergency.

Visors for open face helmets are usually of the fixed wrap-around type, although there are some available that have their own hinges for raising and lowering.

Peaks are often used in conjunction with a visor or goggles, and can offer a fair amount of shade in sunny weather.

Goggles are available in many shapes and sizes and the choice comes down to a personal one. They are usually used in conjunction with an open face helmet, although one or two are available that can be used with a full face helmet.

Gloves

Protection against cold weather and flying stones is very important, so choose a good pair of leather gloves. They are available lined and unlined, with or without knuckle padding and in long or short styles. Make sure they fit properly and are comfortable.

In very cold weather a pair of silk inner gloves is a very worthwhile investment.

Leather is not waterproof so you will need a pair of overmitts for riding in the rain. They are available in nylon or waxed-cotton, the latter being by far the best, but also the more expensive. Nylon tends to slip on the handlebars and soon loses its protective qualities with the constant flexing of the hands.

Boots

A good pair of leather boots will provide support for your ankles, and protection against stones for your shins. Buy a pair with good heavy duty soles. They will last longer and give you better grip when you have to put your feet down.

In wet weather you will need rubber boots or rubber overboots. Leather boots will only provide protection against a light shower. They are not waterproof.

Oversuits

In order to stay dry, warm and comfortable whilst riding you should choose your oversuit with great care. The most popular style is the two-piece, because the jacket can be worn all the time, and the trousers put on when required. One piece suits are ideal for carrying in fine weather in case of a shower, but most are unlined and not really suitable for general use.

The two materials widely used for motorcycle oversuits are nylon and waxed-cotton. Nylon is the most popular, and a good suit is capable of withstanding some very cold and wet weather. It is clean in use and ideal for the commuter.

Waxed-cotton is very tough and hard wearing, as well as being very protective in the worst of weathers. Its one drawback is that it is very greasy to the touch, and tends to make shirt collars and cuffs dirty.

Make sure the suit you decide on is a good fit, allowing enough room for extra clothing in very cold weather.

Leathers

Under normal riding conditions a set of leathers will offer a fair degree of protection against gravel rash and loss of skin in the event of an accident. Cost is the main drawback, with a good set costing up to four times as much as a good oversuit. Leathers are not waterproof, so you will still need to buy some other form of weather protection.

PART TWO
The Law

Section Six
Basic Requirements

Driving Licence

Before you are allowed to ride on the road you must hold a driving licence for the class of vehicle you intend to use. As a learner rider you will need a provisional licence for either a motorcycle or a moped. Remember that the minimum age for riding a motorcycle is 17, while for a moped it is 16.

As the holder of a provisional licence you can only carry a pillion passenger on your motorcycle if that passenger is the holder of a full licence for that class of vehicle. It is not enough for him to have passed his test and hold a certificate of competence to drive. It must be a **full** licence.

Insurance

Very expensive, but very necessary. You are required by law to be covered by at least third party cover.

If you are buying your bike on hire purchase you will only be able to have comprehensive cover, thus protecting the finance company's money.

Test Certificate

If your bike is three years or more old, you must have a current test certificate to show that it is roadworthy.

Vehicle Excise Licence (Tax Disc)

Every vehicle used on the road must display a current excise licence. In the case of a motorcycle or moped it should be displayed on the front lefthand side, and readily visible.

Drink and Drugs

The various laws governing the use of vehicles on our roads are numerous, but obeying the rules in the Highway Code will keep you from falling foul of them. One law that does require a special mention however is the one relating to

19

driving whilst under the influence of drink or drugs.

Drink and drugs do not make your reactions sharper. Even the smallest amount can slow you down enough to make you a hazard on the roads.

NEVER DRINK AND DRIVE.

'L' plates

As a learner rider you must display 'L' plates to both the front and rear of your machine. They should be displayed fully and clearly, and must be the right size – 7in × 7in (178mm × 178mm). It is not legal to wrap the plates around fork legs.

If there is no room to display the plates properly on the bike itself you can make up a board and bracket which can be attached to the machine. The 'L' plate can then be attached to the board.

The front 'L' plate should be clearly displayed, the most common place being just in front of the instruments

The rear 'L' plate must also be clearly displayed, and is usually mounted just below the rear number plate

Section Seven
Maintenance Requirements

Legal requirements for roadworthy machines

Brakes – *must be maintained in an efficient working order*

Lights – *all lights, including stop lamp and indicators, must be clean and working*

Tyres – *must be maintained at their correct pressures, and tread depth must be at least 1mm*

Mudguards – *every motorcycle used on the road must be equipped with front and rear mudguards*

Petrol Tank – *must be made of metal – it is illegal to use a fibre-glass tank on the road*

Rear Footrests – *if a pillion passenger is carried, there must be adequate footrests fitted*

Exhaust – *every exhaust must have a silencer fitted and this must be kept in an efficient working order*

Suspension – *both front and rear suspension units must be in an efficient working order*

Speedometer – *every motorcycle over 100cc must have a working speedometer*

Steering – *the steering system, head bearings, etc., must be maintained in an efficient working order*

PART THREE
On the Road

Section Eight

Riding Position

Comfort is an important factor in road safety, so take your time sorting out your riding position. Handlebars, footrests and other controls can all be moved and adjusted to suit individual requirements.

As a learner, or first time buyer, you should avoid the racing type position offered by some bikes fitted with clip-on bars and rear-set footrests. Control is very

Turn the brake pedal on its locating splines until if falls directly beneath your foot in a normal riding position.

Turn the gear pedal on its splines until it can be operated with a minimum of foot movement.

limited at slow speeds, sometimes even to the point of being dangerous.

Section Nine

Operation of Controls

Motorcycles

Before taking to the roads you should learn how to pull away from a standstill at your local training centre or on waste land.

Having started the machine, and with it in neutral, you should be sitting astride it with both feet on the ground. Pull in the clutch lever with your left hand and raise your left foot to the footrest. Select first gear. Now place your left foot back on the ground and move your right foot to the footrest, with the ball of the foot covering the rear brake pedal.

In order to make the bike move you must now raise the engine speed slightly by turning the throttle twistgrip, and at the same time slowly let out the clutch lever until the bike starts to move forward. At this stage you can leave your feet dragging on the floor to help you keep your balance. Hold the clutch at this point, and repeat the procedure several times in order to get used to the 'feel' of the clutch.

After practising a few times you will soon find the best combination of engine speed and clutch lever movement for perfect starts.

When the bike is actually moving you can slowly let the clutch lever all the way out. You will then be moving along in first gear, and the more you open the throttle the faster you will go within the range of that gear ratio.

With the bike moving at less than 10mph you will find it very difficult to keep your balance when you first start riding, so do not be frightened to exceed this speed. In the chapter on manoeuvring you will find help in achieving good balance.

Auto Mopeds

What could be easier? No clutch to worry about, or gear pedal to mess with. With the engine running, you simply sit astride the machine and open the throttle twistgrip. The more you increase the speed of the engine the faster the bike will go.

Machines with very little engine power, usually only very old ones, may need the assistance of a bit of pedalling to move away from a standstill.

Moving Off On the Road

Before pulling away from the side of the road you must always look behind you. It is not enough to merely glance in your mirrors. A proper rear check is required.

Give a clear right arm signal, lasting about 2 or 3 seconds. Return your right hand to the throttle and switch on your right-hand flashing indicator (if fitted).

Have a further look over your shoulder. Do not rely on your mirrors, and move off only if it is safe to do so. This final check is known as the 'Lifesaver', and it can do just what it says.

Unless you are on a steep down gradient, always use first gear for moving off.

Section Ten

Changing Gear

Gear changes on a motorcycle are achieved by raising or depressing the gear pedal, usually located on the lefthand side of the machine near the footrest. Use the ball of the foot to make down changes, and hook your foot under the pedal and lift it to make up changes. Down for down, up for up.

As speed increases it will become necessary to select a higher gear ratio. After pulling away from a standstill in first you must change to second, then third, etc. It follows that as speed decreases it becomes necessary to change to a lower gear in order to keep the machine moving well. Opening the throttle in too high a gear will result in the bike juddering and possibly even stalling.

The gearbox should also be used when climbing or descending a hill. In order to climb a hill at a steady speed it will be necessary to change to a lower gear and

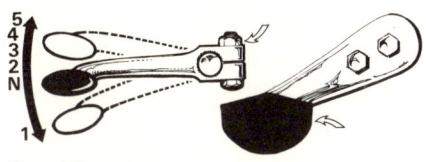

Gear Changing
The most common layout for gear changing is known as 'one down, four up' for a five-speed gearbox. It means that you depress the lever for first gear, and then lift it for other upward changes. After the initial selection of first it becomes 'up' for upward changes, and 'down' for down.

increase the engine speed to avoid the engine labouring.

When descending a steep hill select a lower gear and use engine braking to help slow you down. This will avoid continued use of the brakes which could overheat and eventually fail.

Don't forget that each time you change gear you must pull in the clutch lever and decrease the engine speed slightly. When changing down it may help to 'blip' the throttle as the clutch is pulled in, thus producing a smoother change.

Section Eleven

Stopping

Having learnt how to get your bike on the move you will want to practise stopping it safely. Don't practise on the roads though, use your local training centre or piece of wasteland.

The front brake is the more powerful one and can be used for very heavy braking. There is a fear among new riders that they will go over the top if they put the front brake on too hard, but this is unfounded. The front brake should be used with confidence.

The rear brake is used for additional braking and to help maintain perfect balance.

In dry weather on a good firm road surface you should try to

Machine Under Braking
Under heavy braking the weight of a motorcycle is transferred forward to front wheel. It causes the front suspension to compress, and the rear units to extend. The opposite applies under acceleration.

regulate your braking pressures so that you have 75 per cent front and 25 per cent rear for optimum performance.

In wet conditions, or on a loose road surface you should aim to achieve 50/50 braking.

The front brake must always be applied fractionally before the rear to avoid skidding. Remember that a skidding tyre is not an efficient way of stopping and may result in the machine becoming uncontrollable. Never lock the wheels.

Under normal braking try to change down through the gearbox at the same time. This will leave you in the correct gear after braking is complete, and the extra engine braking will assist the bike to slow down.

The clutch should be left engaged during braking, and only

pulled in and held during the last few feet.

When the bike is almost at a standstill ease off the pressure on the brakes to avoid a harsh jerky stop.

Never brake on a bend. The bike should be upright and travelling in a straight line, otherwise it will be difficult to retain control. If an emergency does arise whilst you are banked over in a bend you may apply light pressure to the rear brake only whilst you bring the bike upright on a straight course to apply heavy braking.

On The Road

Before slowing down you must always check your mirrors, or look over your shoulder, to assess traffic conditions behind. If you are being followed by another vehicle you should inform that driver of your intentions. If there is time, give a slowing down arm signal, but failing that, touch the rear brake pedal just enough to flash the brake light before actually braking.

Emergency Braking

Ideally you should never be in such a position as to need emergency braking, but the ideal is very rare so you must be prepared.

The normal guidelines for braking should be observed, although there will be an obvious need for heavy pressure on both brakes. In a real emergency do not worry about stalling the engine – concentrate on stopping.

Stopping Distances

Mph	(Kph)	Thinking Distance (ft)	(m)	Braking Distance (ft)	(m)	Overall Stopping Distance (ft)	(m)
30	(48)	30	(9.1)	45	(13.7)	75	(22.8)
40	(65)	40	(12.2)	80	(24.3)	120	(36.5)
50	(80)	50	(15.2)	125	(38.1)	175	(53.3)
60	(97)	60	(18.2)	180	(54.8)	240	(73.0)
70	(113)	70	(21.3)	245	(74.6)	315	(95.9)

The above figures are quoted for an alert driver, with good brakes on a dry firm road surface. In wet or adverse conditions you must at least double these distances. Always allow enough room between you and the vehicle in front. If he stops so must you. Work on the principle of leaving one yard (0.9m) for every mph (1.6kph) you are travelling: e.g. 50 yards (45.7m) at 50mph (80.4kph) in dry conditions.

If a vehicle overtakes you and reduces the gap between you and the vehicle in front, drop back and lengthen the space again.

Section Twelve

Riding Drill

Remember	MIRROR SIGNAL MANOEUVRE (MSM)
Mirror	Check your mirrors to assess the situation behind (look over your shoulder if your bike does not have mirrors fitted).
Signal	If you have to alter course or speed give the appropriate signal to warn other road users of your intentions.
Manoeuvre	Check behind again (Lifesaver) before making your manoeuvre, whatever it is.

Section Thirteen

Manoeuvring

In order to perfect your balance and make you a safer low speed rider practise riding in and out of cones placed on the ground. Suggested layouts are given in the accompanying diagrams.

To ride very slowly it will be necessary to slip the clutch rather than have it fully engaged. This is done by holding it at the point where it bites, or first takes up the drive.

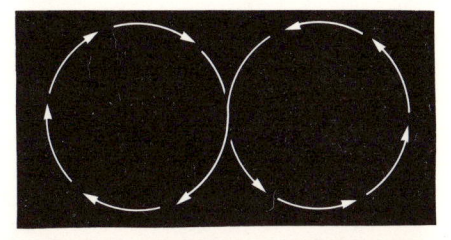

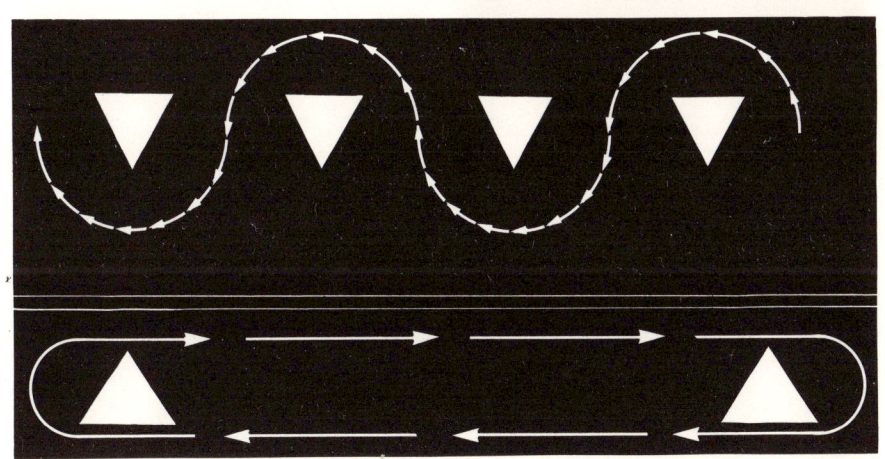

Manoeuvring
In order to learn correct balance and control on your motorcycle you should practise riding around objects. The three diagrams give examples of the layouts you could use. Practise with the objects set fairly wide to start with, and then tighten things up as you become more proficient. It is not part of your test, but will help you to ride better in heavy traffic situations. Good motorcycle control is half the battle!

Section Fourteen

Arm Signals

Left Turn Arm Signal
Raise the left arm from the shoulder to a position parallel to the road surface. It should be given for about 2-3 seconds.

Right Turn Arm Signal
Raise the right arm from the shoulder to a position parallel to the road surface. It should be given for about 2-3 seconds.

Slowing Down Signal
From a point just below the position for a right arm signal, make up and down movements with the arm straight. The palm should face downwards

Turning Left

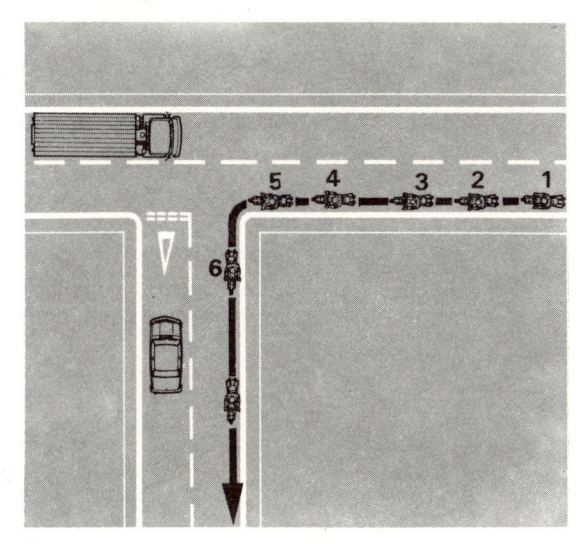

Left Turn Procedure
1. Check behind
2. Arm and indicator signal
3. Check behind, brake to speed required and select the gear for the speed decided upon
4. Check behind and give a confirmation signal if required
5. Lifesaver
6. Cancel indicator

The left turn is probably the easiest of all junction manoeuvres but it still requires your maximum concentration.

On the approach to the turning you will be in the normal riding position on the road, approximately 3ft (1m) from the kerb, depending on road conditions. Well before you intend to make your turn you should look over your right shoulder to assess the traffic situation behind. It is not enough to merely check your mirrors. Give the appropriate arm signal for 2 or 3 seconds, and on returning your hand to the handlebars switch on the left turn flashing indicator (if fitted). Check behind again before adjusting your speed to that required to negotiate the corner, and select the appropriate gear for the speed decided upon.

Check behind again, and if necessary, give a further left arm signal to confirm your intentions. The final stage before actually turning is the Lifesaver, and in the case of the left turn this is done by looking over the left shoulder to make sure the manoeuvre can be made in complete safety.

Never swing out before actually turning, and try to maintain your 3ft (1m) from the kerb position after the turn has been completed.

29

Section Sixteen

Turning Right

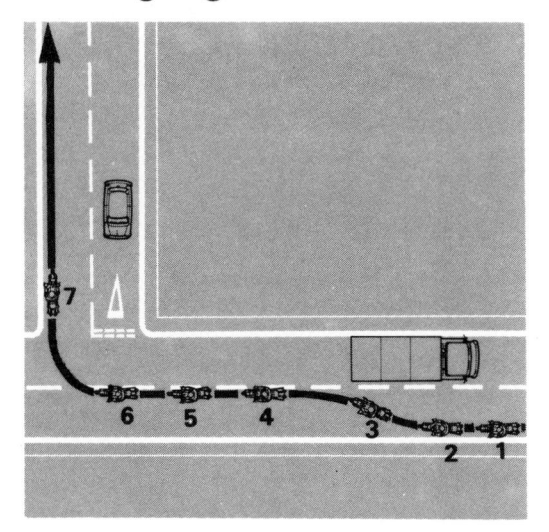

Right Turn Procedure
1. Check behind and give right arm and indicator signal
2. Check behind
3. Move gradually to crown of road if safe to do so
4. Check behind, brake to speed required and select the gear for the speed decided upon
5. Check behind and give confirmation signal if necessary
6. Lifesaver
7. Cancel indicator

This, the more dangerous of the two turns, is quite straightforward if the following procedure is undertaken.

Give yourself plenty of time on the approach to be able to carry out all the safety checks. Look over your right shoulder to assess the situation behind well before the turning. You should at this point be travelling approximately 3ft (1m) from the kerb. Give a right arm signal for about 2 or 3 seconds, and on returning your hand to the handlebars switch on the right-hand flashing indicator (if fitted). Check behind again and if it is safe to do so, start to manoeuvre to a position just left of the crown of the road.

When you are back on a straight course look behind again before adjusting your speed to that required to negotiate the corner. Select the correct gear for the speed decided upon. Check behind again and give a further right arm signal if necessary to confirm your intentions.

The final check is the Lifesaver, and in the case of the right turn it is made over the right shoulder to make sure that the manoeuvre can be completed in safety.

Be prepared to stop and give way to oncoming traffic, and after making the turn return to the normal position on the road of 3ft (1m) from the kerb.

If you are turning out of a side road into a main road it will be controlled by either a STOP or GIVE WAY sign. In these cases you should stop and give way as required, but do not forget to look right, then left, then right again before moving off when it is safe to do so.

Section Seventeen

Crossroads

Negotiating crossroads is one of the most dangerous manoeuvres carried out by a motorcyclist, especially in heavy traffic. Drivers of other vehicles seem to have difficulty in seeing, or assessing the speed of, approaching bikes. You must exercise the utmost care, check everything and not rely on luck or the other person.

You are put at risk by vehicles in front of you, behind you, to your left and right, and any or all could have you off! Good observation on your approach, and whilst crossing the crossroads, is essential.

Use your horn if you don't think a particular driver has seen you. You are not being aggressive, merely telling him of your presence. Don't rely on the driver hearing your horn. He may be deaf, or have his car radio turned up very high.

Crossroads in country areas are not always marked out for priorities so extreme caution must be exercised. Never assume that you have right of way. The other driver might be doing just the same. Use of the horn, or flashing the headlight after dark, will help to warn others of your presence, but again don't rely on it and think it is okay to just give a toot and carry on.

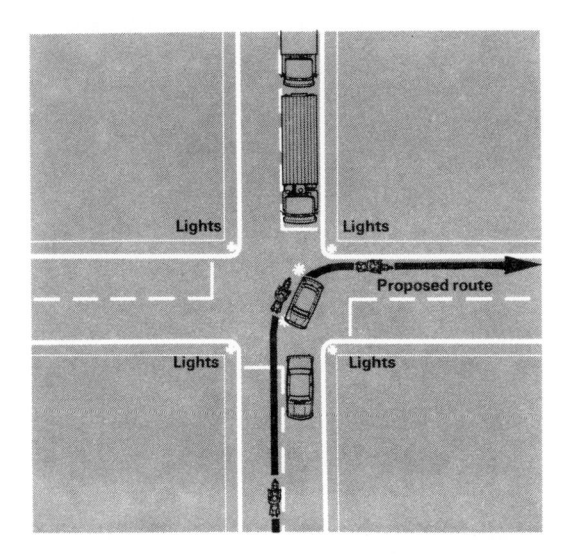

Negotiating Crossroads
All crossroads, whether controlled by traffic lights or not, should be treated with extreme caution, regardless of who has right of way. Be on the lookout for somebody doing something wrong – 'amber gamblers', etc. Remember to pass 'offside' to 'offside'.

If the crossroads are slightly offset you must not try to straighten them out. Follow the intended line of the traffic. If you cross the opposite stop or give-way lines you could fail your test

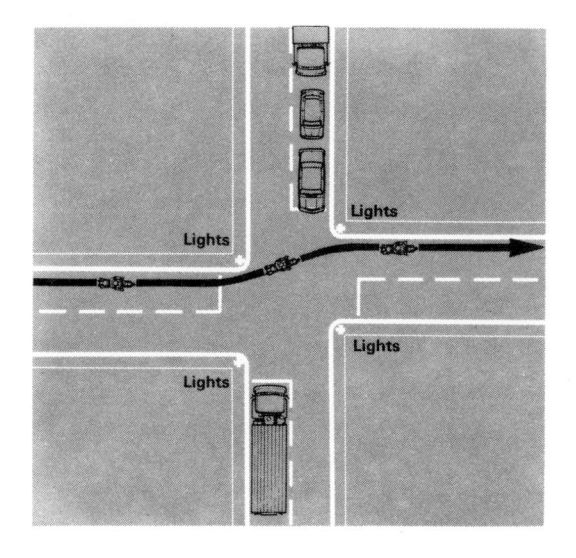

Section Eighteen

Entering Main Roads

Every time you enter a main road you will be faced with a different situation, so be prepared. Junction layouts differ, as do weather and traffic conditions. Never take anything for granted, even if you know the junction.

You will either have to stop or give way at the junction with the main road, depending on the road sign and road markings. If it is a GIVE WAY sign and you can see that all is clear to proceed then you need not actually stop, but if you are in any doubt whatsoever you must stop and check.

The main road you are about to enter may have a 60 or 70mph speed limit, so be prepared for vehicles approaching you at such speeds.

Make use of any slip lanes provided for joining main roads. They are used to increase your speed before filtering into the other traffic to join the main carriageway.

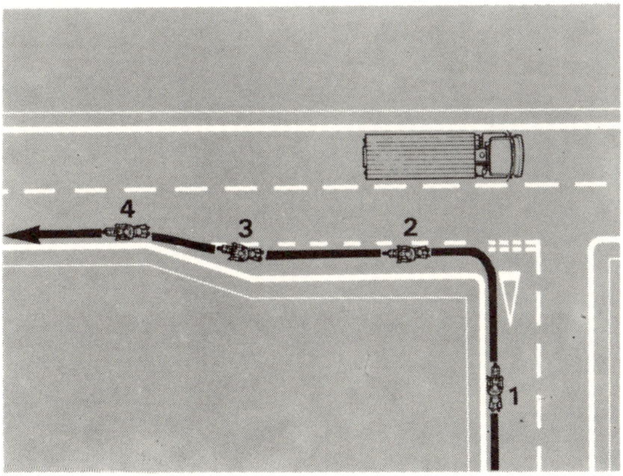

1. Approach as for normal left turn
2. Join slip lane and check over right shoulder. Adjust speed to other traffic, but also be prepared to stop. Right hand indicator
3. Lifesaver – over right shoulder
4. Take up normal riding position and cancel indicator

Section Nineteen

Roundabouts

General

On the approach to a roundabout, check the road direction signs for the layout of the junction. Note the exit you require so that you can take up a correct position on the road in plenty of time and give the appropriate signal.

Give way to traffic coming from your right as you enter the roundabout. This is a legal requirement.

Maintain lane discipline whilst actually negotiating the roundabout. Remember – on a two lane carriageway if you enter by the nearside lane leave by the nearside lane, if you enter by the offside lane you must leave by the offside lane.

Straight Ahead

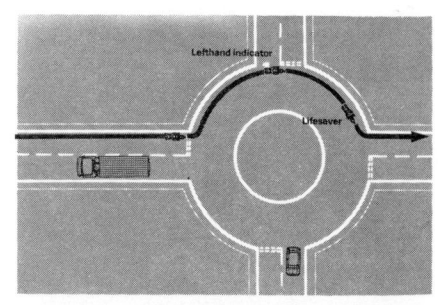

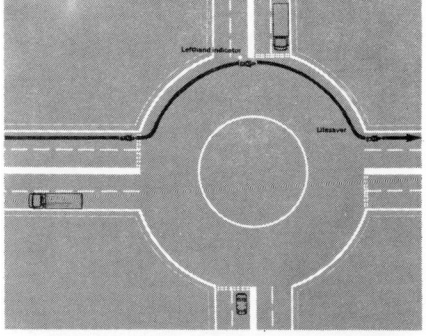

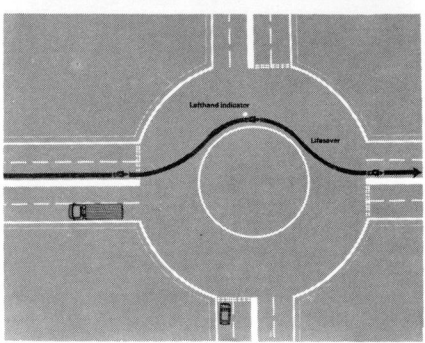

The normal approach to a roundabout when you intend to ride straight ahead will be near to the lefthand kerb. Check the traffic situation behind on your approach by looking over your right shoulder. Slow the bike down using brakes and gears until you are travelling at the right speed to negotiate the junction, and select the right gear for that speed.

Watch the traffic already on the roundabout, giving way to those approaching from the right, and filter in, keeping to the lefthand side of the lane. Give a left turn signal when you are passing the exit before the one you require. Before actually leaving the roundabout you should look over your left shoulder (Lifesaver). Other vehicles have a habit of creeping up on the inside.

Left Turn

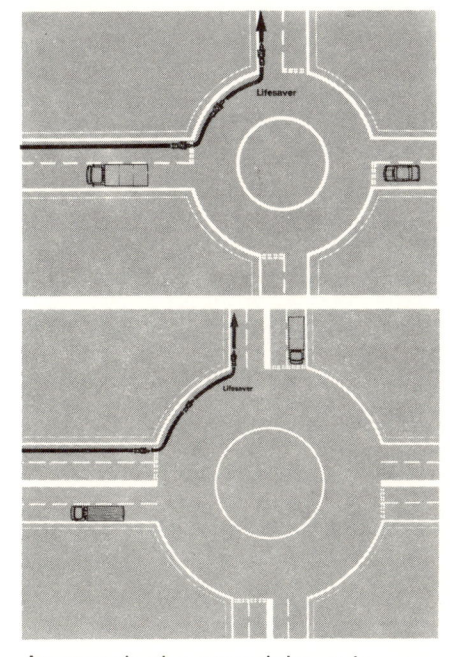

Approach the roundabout in your normal position on the road, approximately 3ft (1m) from the nearside kerb. Check behind, by looking over your shoulder, well before the turning, and assess the situation behind. Give a left arm signal for about 2 or 3 seconds, and on returning your hand to the handlebars switch on the lefthand flashing indicator.

Check behind again before reducing your speed to that required. Select the correct gear for the speed decided upon.

Check behind again and if necessary give a left arm confirmation signal.

Watch the traffic already on the roundabout. Give way to traffic approaching from the right and be prepared to stop. Before actually leaving at your exit look over your left shoulder (Lifesaver).

Right Turn

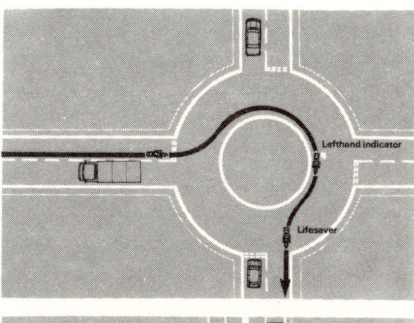

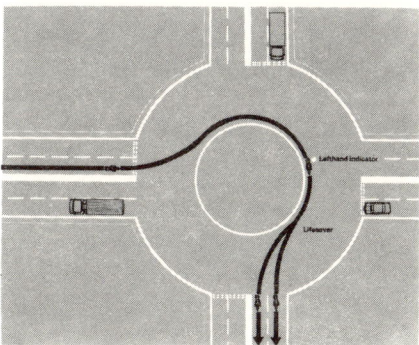

On the approach to the roundabout you should take up a position either near to the crown of

35

the road as for a normal right turn, or in the offside lane of a two lane road. Give a right arm signal which can then be supplemented by a righthand flashing indicator. Rear shoulder checks will probably best be made over the left shoulder because of your position out to the right.

Give way to taffic approaching from the right as you filter into the flow of traffic. Maintain a position close to the roundabout or in the offside lane. As you pass the exit before the one you require change from a righthand flashing indicator to a left one, check over your left shoulder and prepare to leave at your exit. Just prior to actually leaving the roundabout have a final look over your left shoulder (Lifesaver). Beware of traffic travelling on your nearside.

Section Twenty

Dual Carriageways

Under normal riding conditions a dual carriageway should be treated as just a wide road. Keep to the nearside lane except when overtaking, and then move well out towards the central reservation giving yourself plenty of room for safety.

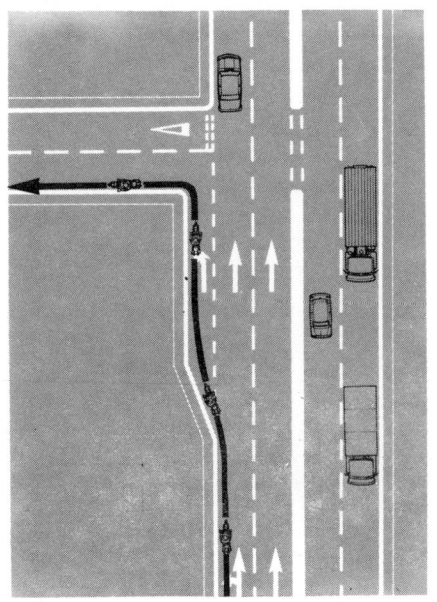

Left Turns

The normal procedure for a left turn should be carried out at all times, but watch for exit slip roads. They are used to reduce your speed without inconvenience to following traffic and the risk of being hit from behind.

Right Turns

Again the standard procedure should be undertaken on the

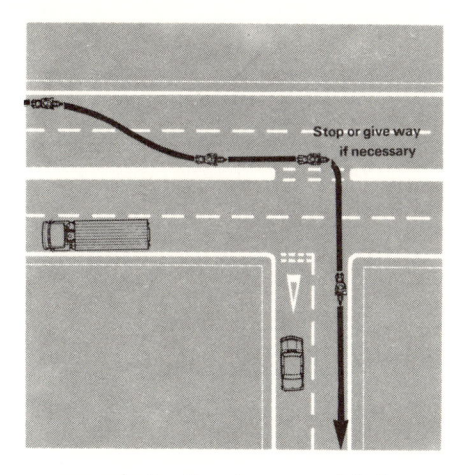

first carriageway and place yourself within the area of the central reserve, then cross the second carriageway when safe to do so.

The same applies to turning right onto a dual carriageway. Treat it as two individual roads (see below).

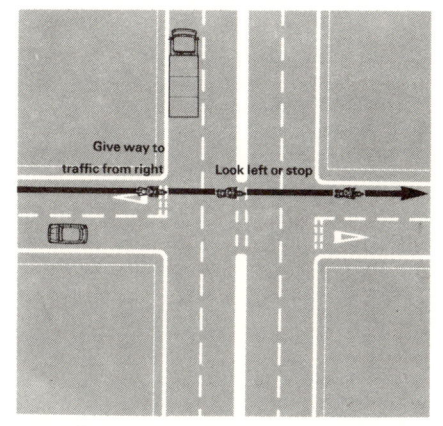

approach to the turn, and full use should be made of any slip roads in the central reserve.

Crossing Dual Carriageways

Treat each part of a dual carriageway as a separate road. Cross the

Section Twenty-One

Gradients

The use of the gearbox for travelling up and down hills has been explained on page 25. It should also be borne in mind that when descending a steep winding hill to brake only when travelling straight, and not actually in the bends.

Hill Starts

To hold the bike stationary on a hill you will need to apply either the front or rear brake. When you are ready to move off, sit with both your feet on the ground, using the front brake to stop it rolling backwards. Raise your left foot to the footrest and select first gear. Replace your left foot on the ground and raise your right foot to its footrest. Hold the back brake on with your right foot and release the front brake. Raise the engine speed by turning the throttle, and at the same time ease out the clutch lever until the engine begins to bite. The bike will feel as though it wants to move but is being held back. Slowly release your pressure on the foot brake and the machine will start to move forward.

Parking

When it is necessary to park on a hill the following should be remembered: Motorcycle stands, both centrestands and sidestands, work in an almost vertical position and rely on the weight of the bike being slightly to the rear of the stand. If you park your machine facing downhill there is a possibility that the weight transfer forward will cause it to roll off the stand.

Always park facing uphill to avoid this.

Hill 1 in 5

Top Gear 5th

4th

3rd

4th

If you are travelling along in top gear, and are faced with an up gradient, you should be prepared to change to a lower gear, depending on the incline. If you maintain top gear on a steep slope the bike will slow down to a point where it will eventually stall because of the load put on it

Section Twenty-Two

Pedestrian Crossings

Zebra Crossings

Pedestrians actually on a Zebra Crossing have the right of way, so you must always approach them at a speed low enough to be able to stop if necessary. Check behind you on your approach and if necessary give a slowing down signal to warn following traffic, which may not be able to see the crossing clearly, of your intentions.

Let the pedestrian decide when it is safe to cross. If you intend to stop and give way your slowing down signal will inform them. Never call the pedestrian across. They must judge themselves when it is safe to cross.

Zig-Zags

The zig-zag areas of pedestrian crossings serve two main purposes; indicating no parking and no overtaking. You are not allowed to park or wait anywhere within the zig-zags, and you must not overtake a vehicle on the approach side of the crossing.

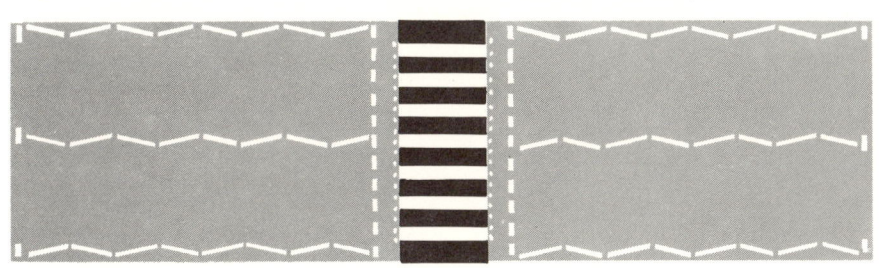

Zebra controlled areas

39

Central Islands

Crossings which have central pedestrian islands should be treated as two separate crossings. You do not have to give way to pedestrians on the crossing on the other side of the island.

Pelican Crossings

You should treat all crossings controlled by traffic lights in exactly the same way as you would treat traffic lights at a junction. You must stop when either the steady amber or red lights show. The only difference in operation is that the Pelican Crossings have a flashing amber light instead of red and amber.

The flashing amber light means that you must give way to pedestrians, but if it is all clear you may proceed.

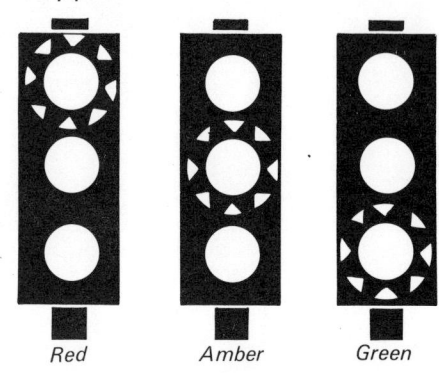

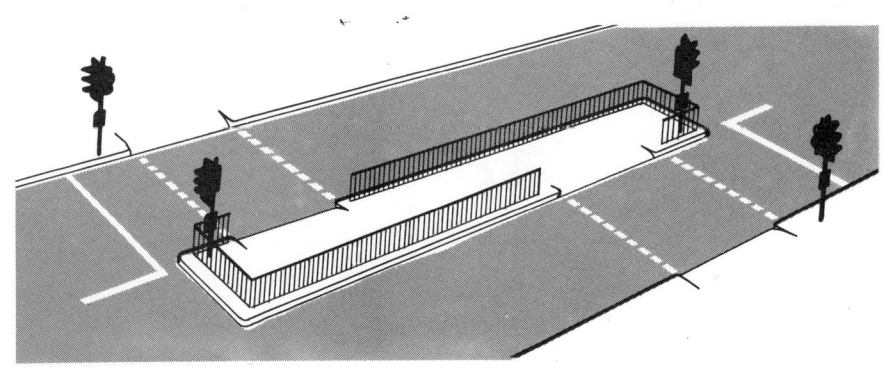

Red   Amber   Green

Treat Pelican crossings with great care. You will find that pedestrians will run on to the crossing when the lights indicate that the traffic has the right of way. Always approach them at a speed slow enough for you to stop if the lights change to red against you. It is an offence to cross the red light

Section Twenty-Three

Overtaking

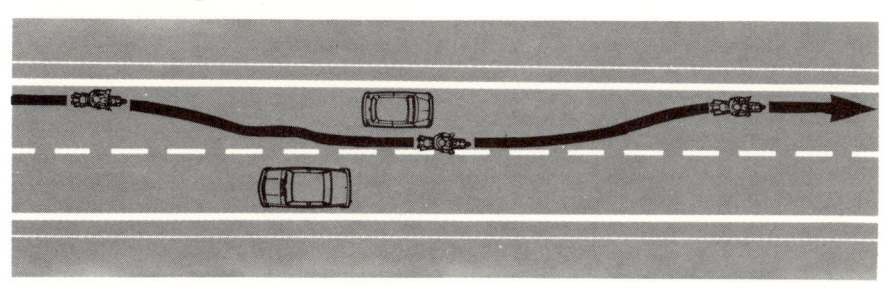

Never overtake unless it is necessary and completely safe to do so. You will be travelling on the wrong side of the road and at risk all the time.

Well before you intend to overtake another moving vehicle check behind by looking over your right shoulder, and assess traffic conditions. Take up a position on the road well behind the vehicle you intend to overtake, and out towards the centre of the road so that you can see well in front. If you are not clear of what lies ahead move over to the nearside and check along the inside of the vehicle.

Check behind again before selecting the correct gear to give you the acceleration for the manoeuvre. Give a right signal and a final check behind (Lifesaver). Overtake as quickly as possible and return to your normal position on the road.

Care should be taken to assess the speed of following and oncoming traffic.

Always allow more than the width of a car door for every overtaking manoeuvre

41

Highway Code

The Highway Code lists several places where it is dangerous to overtake. Learn them.

Never overtake – if you have to cross double white lines, or where the unbroken line is nearest to you.

Never overtake – within the zig-zag approach to a pedestrian crossing.

Never overtake – when you see a 'no overtaking' sign

Do not overtake – at or when coming to the brow of a hill, corner or bend, hump-back bridge, road junction, level crossing, pedestrian crossing, diagonal stripes on the road surface or where to do so would force another vehicle to slow down or alter course.
IF IN ANY DOUBT – HOLD BACK – DO NOT OVERTAKE.

Stationary Vehicles

Parked vehicles can hide many dangers for the motorcyclist, including pedestrians and the opening of car doors. Always give them plenty of room, at least 4ft (1.2m) or about the width of an open door. It is quite acceptable in the interests of safety to move out to the wrong side of the road, providing there is nothing coming in the opposite direction.

A position well out to the right will give you a better point for observation between the vehicles. Look for legs, small wheels, dogs, cats, or anything else that could be a danger.

Remember to check behind you before making any alteration to your course or speed, and do not forget to check over your left shoulder before returning to the nearside of the road (Lifesaver).

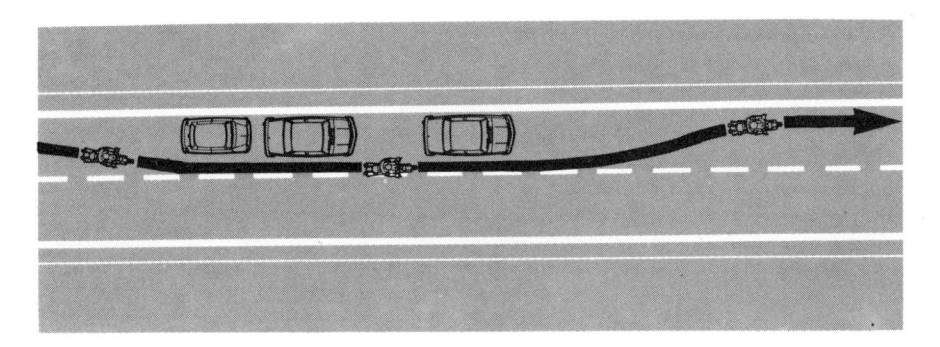

Section Twenty-Four

Night Riding

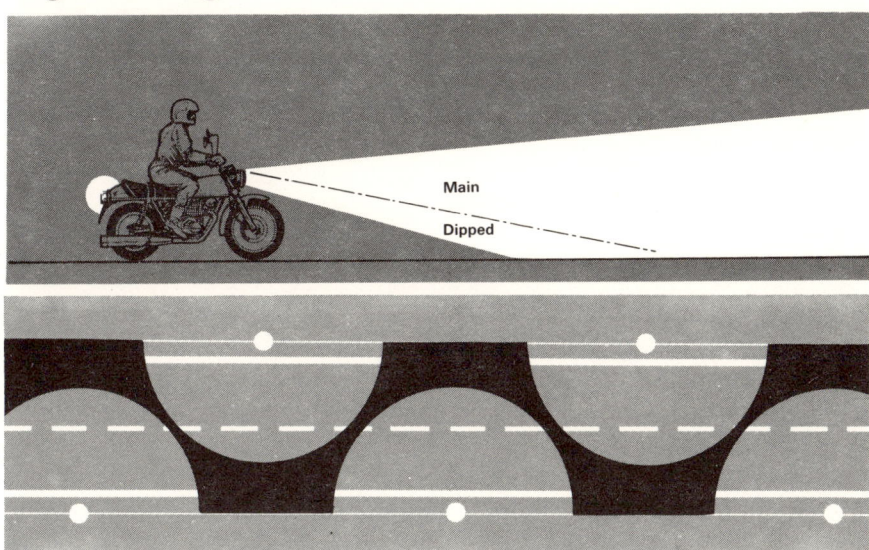

Always ride on dipped beam, or main beam, during the hours of darkness. Never ride on your pilot light alone. Follow those two rules and you will see and be seen at night.

Even in brightly lit town centres you should use your dipped beam. You will not run your battery down, as many people think.

The main beam should be used whenever the dipped beam is not powerful enough in dark conditions to light up the road ahead, but remember to dip the light for oncoming traffic and when riding behind someone else. Glare from oncoming lights can be very distracting, and can cause accidents.

If you are dazzled by oncoming lights do not retaliate by switching yours to main beam. Slow down and if necessary stop. Never look directly into the lights, but always to one side.

Street Lighting

Modern street lighting is very good, with each pool of light overlapping to form a continuous illuminated area. Old street lighting, however, is not as powerful. The pools of light are spaced by areas of darkness which can hide many dangers; parked cars, potholes, etc.

Visors

Always make sure that your visor is clean and clear when riding at night, and NEVER use a tinted visor. They do not reduce glare, only your range of vision.

Section Twenty-Five

Adverse Conditions

Remember the maxim – SEE AND BE SEEN. Always use your dipped headlight in adverse weather conditions, it is not only a legal requirement, but also a safety one.

Your speed must always be reduced to match the prevailing conditions, and you must allow extra room between yourself and the vehicle in front.

Rain

Wet roads can be very slippery, especially after a long dry period. Oil dropped by other vehicles is not washed away and many roads become skid pans. Slow down and treat the road with respect.

In wet conditions you may find your visor misting up, thus restricting your vision. At low speed and in light rain you can lift your visor which will then act as a peak, deflecting much of the water away. In heavy rain or at speed this will not work so you must take prior precautions. Various anti-mist products are on the market but they tend to be expensive, and ordinary washing up liquid wiped across the inside of the visor will serve just as well.

Fog

The ideal situation in thick fog is to stay at home, but if you must go out take extra care. Only use dipped headlights, because the main beam will tend to bounce off the fog and cause glare.

Never rely on the vehicle in front to show you the way. He could be heading straight for the canal! Travel at a speed that you can see in front far enough for safety.

Raise your visor, or treat it as previously outlined, so that you can see. If you do keep your visor down remember it will mist up on the outside as well.

SLOW DOWN AND KEEP YOUR DISTANCE.

Snow

Normally when snow falls it turns to water on contact with the road so riding conditions are basically the same as in the wet. The snow, however, does tend to collect on visors, windscreens, road signs, etc., making vision for yourself and others very restricted. Slow down and adjust to the conditions.

Fresh, packed snow will offer some grip to motorcycle tyres, but hard packed snow will be as slippery and as lethal as ice.

Remember to use the gearbox to reduce speed and not the brakes, they will only lock the wheel and cause it to slide.

Ice

The ice you can see is the best sort. You know it is there and can adjust your speed and riding technique accordingly. It is the ice you cannot see that causes all the problems. Black ice. We get it every year, and it always catches someone out. On a very cold day when the roads just look wet take extra care, the water on the surface could be hiding a layer of ice.

Section Twenty-Six

Observation

Everything on or alongside our roads is a potential hazard and a danger; other vehicles, pedestrians, lamp-posts, trees, manhole covers, drains, changes in road surface, etc., the list is endless. You should always be looking for these hazards, and be prepared to take the necessary action.

Good observation is essential if you wish to remain safe. Never rush into a situation, hold back and size it up. If in any doubt, stop.

In towns you should be looking for other vehicles, pedestrians, parked vehicles and the dangers they can hide. Manhole covers, drains and road markings are other hazards, particularly in the wet. At blind junctions a shop window can act like a mirror and warn you of the approach of other vehicles.

In the country you should be looking over hedges and across fields to try and determine the course of the road ahead. Telegraph poles can be useful, but be careful, some tend to cut across fields and not follow the road.

Keep well away from loose dirt and rubbish at the side of the road, even if it means crossing to the wrong side of the road. This is of particular importance along country roads

Speed

As you increase speed so you will automatically look further ahead to compensate. There is very little you can do if something happens right in front of you at 70mph, so take a careful note of everything you see well in advance. Make sure the hazard is safe to pass before you reach the point of no return.

45

Section Twenty-Seven

Parking

Motorcycles and mopeds require very little space for parking and you can often make use of a space that is too small for a car. You must obey any parking restrictions because they apply to all road users.

In some towns there are special parking spaces allocated for solo motorcycles. Some are at the side of the road, others are in the middle.

Be careful of road cambers when leaving your machine at the side of the road. It is possible that it could fall over whilst you are away.

Make use of car parks wherever possible. They are safer than leaving your bike at the roadside where it could be damaged by passing vehicles. Read the car park instructions carefully, they vary quite a lot. Some charge for parking solo motorcycles, and some don't provided they are put in the designated place.

Use of any steering lock or anti-theft device fitted will make it harder for any would-be thief.

Section Twenty-Eight

Motorways

As a learner rider you are not allowed to venture onto the motorways, but after passing your test you will probably want to do so. Don't make the mistake of thinking that because you are now qualified as a rider you are automatically a good motorway rider. Take your time. Make one or two short trips on and off, just to get used to the speeds and general conditions.

It is possible to find a dual carriageway with slip roads leading on and off, and it is a good idea to practise the art of joining a motorway on these roads.

Use the slip road to increase your speed to that of the traffic already on the motorway (as shown below), give a right turn signal and filter in. Don't forget the Lifesaver. Settle down to the speed and conditions before mov-

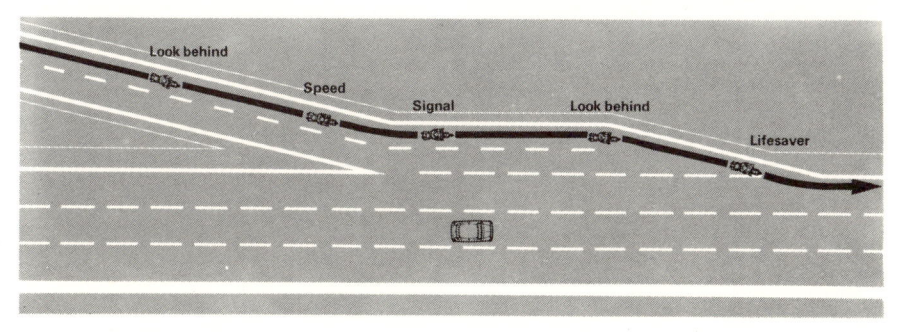

47

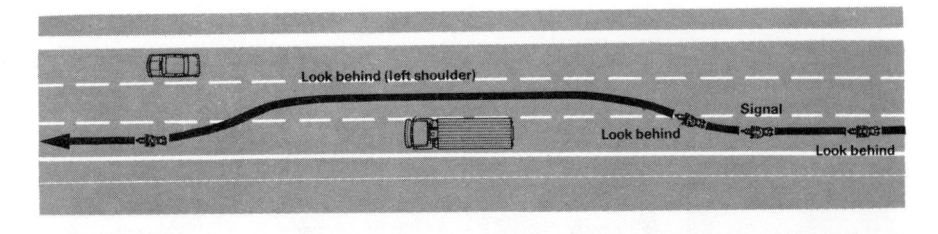

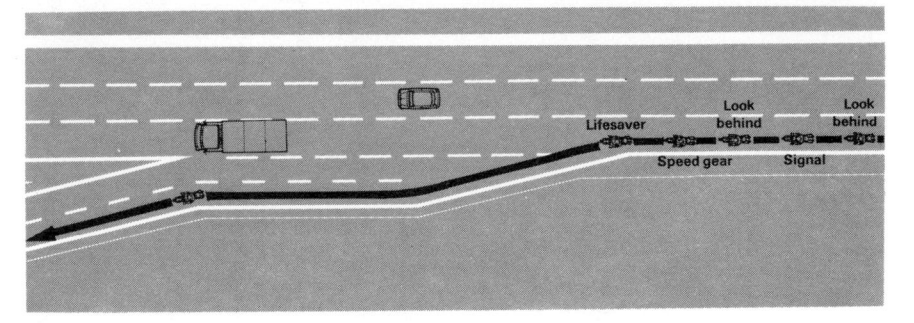

ing to the middle and offside lanes for overtaking (see page 48).

Always give yourself plenty of room to manoeuvre and signal well in advance. Take extra care with your rear view checks – speed can be deceptive.

If you are overtaken by a large lorry be prepared for the rush of air – which will be strong enough to move you about quite a lot, especially if you are on a small machine.

When leaving the motorway use the slip road (see the lower diagram on this page) to adjust your speed to that required for the roads to follow. Keep a watchful eye on your speedometer for the next few miles; it is surprising how easy it is to travel too fast after leaving a motorway.

The Law

There are certain laws regarding the use of motorways. The main ones are all explained in the Highway Code, and some are given on a sign as you join the motorway.

Remember – No motorcycles under 50cc
No learner riders
No stopping or U-turns
In an emergency use the hard shoulder.

The emergency telephones along the side of a motorway are not connected to motoring organisations such as the AA or RAC, but are connected directly to Police control who will deal with your difficulty, whether it be a breakdown or an accident.

PART FOUR
Taking the Test

Section Twenty-Nine

The Test

Since 1 February 1983 the law has required a two-part motorcycle test, and that learner riders be restricted to 125cc machines.

Motorcycle learners must take the two-part test. Part 1 takes place at a Heavy Goods Vehicle Testing Station, and is designed to test control skills around various patterns of cones. It is not possible to apply for Part 2 of the test without a Part 1 pass certificate. The Part 2 test remains as it has always been, an observed ride on public roads, conducted by a DoT examiner.

You must pass your test (both parts) within two years of receiving your provisional driving licence, or suffer a one-year ban. There is no fine or endorsement, but you will not be issued with another provisional licence for 12 months. This ban does not apply if you hold a full car licence, which automatically includes a provisional motorcycle licence, or if you have passed the moped test.

Moped learners do not have to take Part 1 of the test, and are exempt from the 12-month ban rule — they can take as long as they like to pass their test.

The minimum age for riding a motorcycle is 17 (16 for a moped) and learners are restricted to bikes of a maximum of 125cc. If the machine was first registered on or after 1 January 1982 it must also carry a plate stating that it does not exceed 9kW (approx 12bhp). If the bike was first registered before this date there is no power restriction, but it still must not exceed 125cc.

Hints on Taking your Test

Obtain and read thoroughly the leaflet known as the DL 68 or 'Your Driving Test and How to Pass'.

Make sure you have practised everything properly, and know exactly what is required of you. Check the date and time of your test and make sure you are there.

Ride naturally and do not try to show off.

The examiner will be looking for the correct procedures at road junctions and hazards, and also for smooth and confident control of your machine.

You will not be asked any difficult or catch questions, only those which relate to the test as defined in the DL 68 and the Highway Code.

The examiner will know that you are nervous and will allow for this. If you make a mistake don't worry. Carry on, but try not to make the same mistake twice.

Make sure you have enough petrol to complete the test. It won't

49

be very good for your image if you run out half-way through.

Section Thirty

The Highway Code

The following 30 questions are typical of those you may be asked when taking your test.

The answers are on page 51.

Questions

1. What must you do before moving off?
2. When should you give signals?
3. What advice are you given with regards to tinted optical equipment?
4. What is the main 'rule of the road'?
5. Complete the following – Never ride so fast that you cannot stop...
6. What should you do when riding near schools?
7. What is the overall stopping distance from 70mph, as given in rule 47?
8. In addition to parking, the zig-zag areas of a pedestrian crossing control overtaking. What is the rule?
9. What should you do when riding past animals?
10. What do areas of white diagonal stripes or white chevrons on the road surface mean?
11. When can you overtake on the left?
12. What should you do when crossing or turning right into a dual carriageway?
13. What should you do when entering a roundabout?
14. What is the meaning of flashing headlamps?
15. What do you know about the use of the horn?
16. What should you do if the barriers on an automatic level crossing stay down for more than 3 minutes without a train arriving?
17. What does a green traffic light mean?
18. Describe the roadsign for 'No overtaking'.
19. Some roadsigns have circles, others have triangles. Why?
20. When the amber light flashes at a Pelican crossing what should you do?
21. What sign will you find at the entrance to a main road?
22. What is the sequence of the traffic lights, starting at red?
23. What does the flashing amber light at a Pelican crossing mean?
24. What should you do if you are dazzled by the lights of oncoming vehicles?

Motorways

25. If you miss your exit what should you do?
26. What must you not do if you miss your exit?
27. What should you do if you break down or have an accident?
28. What should you do if something falls from your motorcycle?
29. Are the speed limits shown by overhead gantries advisory or mandatory?
30. How do you enter a motorway?

Answers

1. Use your mirrors and check over your shoulder for traffic. Give a signal if necessary. Move off only when it is perfectly safe to do so.
2. Give signals if they would help or warn other road users.
3. Do not use tinted optical equipment of any kind at night or in conditions of poor visibility.
4. Keep to the left, except when road signs or markings indicate otherwise, or when you have to pass stationary vehicles or pedestrians in the road.
5. ...well within the distance you can see to be clear. Ride much more slowly if the road is wet or icy, or if there is fog. Do not brake sharply except in an emergency.
6. Ride slowly and look out for children getting on or off buses. Stop when signalled to do so by a school crossing patrol.
7. 315ft (95.9m) – 70ft (21.3m) thinking distance, 245ft (74.6m) braking distance.
8. On the approach side you must not overtake the moving motor vehicle nearest to the crossing, or the leading vehicle which has stopped to give way to pedestrians crossing.
9. Go slowly, give them plenty of room and be ready to stop if necessary. Do not frighten them with your horn or by revving your engine. Watch out for animals being led on your side of the road and be especially careful at a lefthand bend.
10. They separate streams of traffic liable to be a danger to each other, or protect traffic turning right. Do not ride over these areas if you can avoid doing so.
11. When the driver in front has signalled that he intends to turn right and you can pass without getting in the way of others. When you want to turn left at a junction. When traffic is moving slowly in queues and the vehicles on your right are moving slower than you are. In one-way streets (but not dual carriageways).
12. Treat each half of the dual carriageway as a separate road. Wait in the central dividing strip until there is a safe gap in the traffic on the second half of the road. If the central reserve is not very wide you should aim to make the manoeuvre in one move.
13. Give way to traffic on your immediate right unless road markings indicate otherwise. Keep moving if the way is clear. Keep a special look out for the 'Give Way' lines.
14. They have the same meaning as sounding the horn: to warn other road users of your presence on the road.
15. It is used to warn others of your presence. It should not be used between the hours of 2330 and 0700 in a built-up area, or when your vehicle is stationary (except at times of danger to another vehicle moving).
16. Use the telephone at the crossing to ask the signalman's advice.

17 You may go if the way is clear. Take special care if you mean to turn left or right and give way to pedestrians who are crossing.
18 White circle with red border containing two cars, a black one on the left and a red one on the right.
19 Triangular signs give advanced warning of a hazard ahead. Circular signs may be prohibitions, regulatory or mandatory.
20 You must give way to any pedestrian on the crossing; otherwise you may proceed.
21 Either a 'STOP' or 'GIVE WAY' sign.
22 Red – red and amber – green – amber – red.
23 You must give way to pedestrians on the crossing, otherwise you may proceed.
24 Slow down or stop. Never flash your lights back.

Motorways

25 Continue until you reach the next exit.
26 Do not reverse or turn in the carriageway, or drive against the traffic or cross the central reservation.
27 Get your vehicle onto the hard shoulder as quickly as possible and use the emergency telephone to summon assistance.
28 Use the emergency telephone to call the Police. Do not try to retrieve it yourself.
29 They are advisory, but are put there to help you in the prevailing conditions.
30 From the access point at the end of the slip road, watch for a gap in the traffic in the nearside lane, and give way to traffic already on the motorway. Accelerate in the extra lane and join the nearside lane travelling at the same speed as the traffic already on it.

Section Thirty-One

Do's and Don'ts

DO – make sure your bike is roadworthy

DO – make sure your driving licence is current for that class of vehicle and is signed

DO – adjust the controls of your machine so that you have a comfortable riding position

DO – make sure that you have the proper clothing for the job in hand and the weather conditions prevailing

DO – make sure the bike is in neutral before starting the engine

DO – check behind you before moving off from rest

DO – make regular use of your mirrors and shoulder checks to assess traffic conditions behind

DO – stop if you are involved in an accident, or instructed to do so by a Policeman

DO – read and learn the Highway Code. It is the road user's bible

DO – give clear and adequate signals before making a manoeuvre

DO – be patient with other road users, and never lose your temper

DO NOT – ride if you are tired or unfit through drink or drugs, or if you have a temporary physical disability that will impair 100 per cent control and concentration.

DO NOT – show off in front of others

DO NOT – think you know it all just because you have passed your test, you have only just started learning how to ride a motorcycle

DO NOT – disregard any road sign, they are there for your safety and guidance

DO NOT – race other cars or bikes. It is illegal and dangerous

DO NOT – expect the other person to always do the correct and proper thing. Look for the unexpected

DO NOT – forget that as a motorcyclist you are at a greater risk than the drivers of cars and lorries. Ride defensively and protect yourself as much as possible

DO NOT – ride too close to the vehicle in front, leave enough room so that you can stop if he does

DO NOT – mistreat your motorcycle, it is all that is between you and the road surface

ROAD MARKINGS
Across the carriageway

Give way to traffic on major road

Give way to traffic from right in roundabout

Give way to traffic from right at mini-roundabout

Stop lines at 'Stop' sign

Stop lines at signals or police control

Along the carriageway

Hazard warning lines

Centre line

Lane line

Do not enter marked area

Do not cross solid line if it is on your side

Do not cross double white lines

The time plates must be consulted to find out when the restrictions indicated by the lines apply. If there are no plates the restrictions apply on every day

Examples of plates indicating restriction times

Mon-Sat 8 am-6.30 pm
Plate giving times

At any time
Continuous prohibition

Mon - Sat 8 am - 6 pm Waiting Limited to 20 minutes Return prohibited within 40 minutes
Limited waiting

During every working day

During every working day and additional times

During any other periods

The plates show when the restrictions apply. If there are no plates the restrictions apply on every day

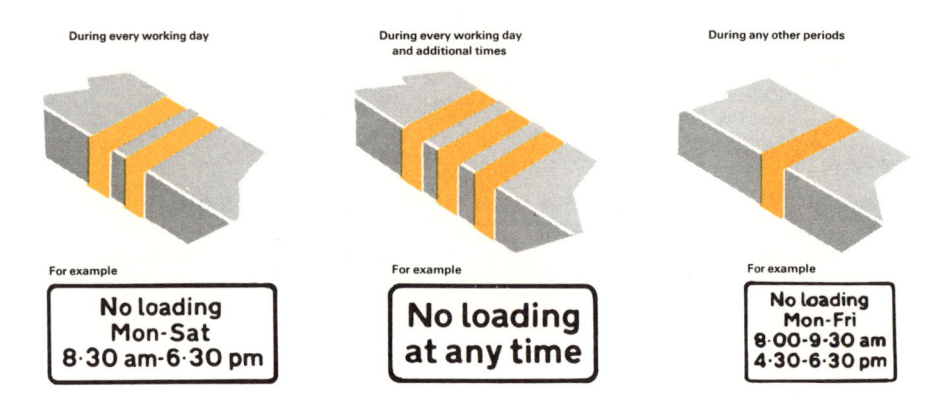

During every working day

During every working day and additional times

During any other periods

For example
No loading
Mon-Sat
8.30 am-6.30 pm

For example
No loading
at any time

For example
No loading
Mon-Fri
8.00-9.30 am
4.30-6.30 pm

Keep entrance clear of stationary vehicles, even if picking up or setting down children

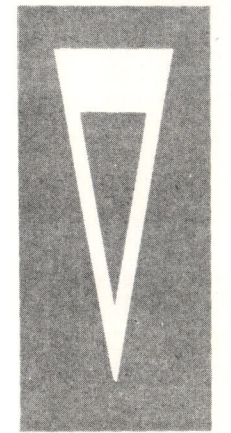

'Give Way' warning just ahead

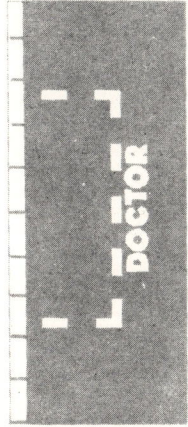

Parking space reserved for named vehicles

Bus stop

Bus lane

Box junction

Do not block entrance to side road

Indication of traffic lanes

Roadside signals

Temporary maximum speed

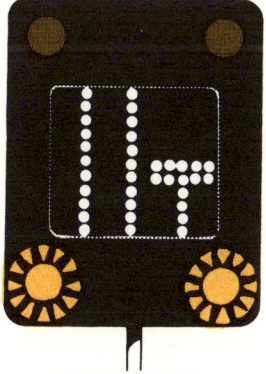

Lane closed ahead

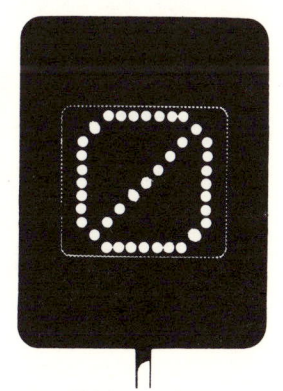

End of restriction

57

TRAFFIC LIGHT SIGNALS

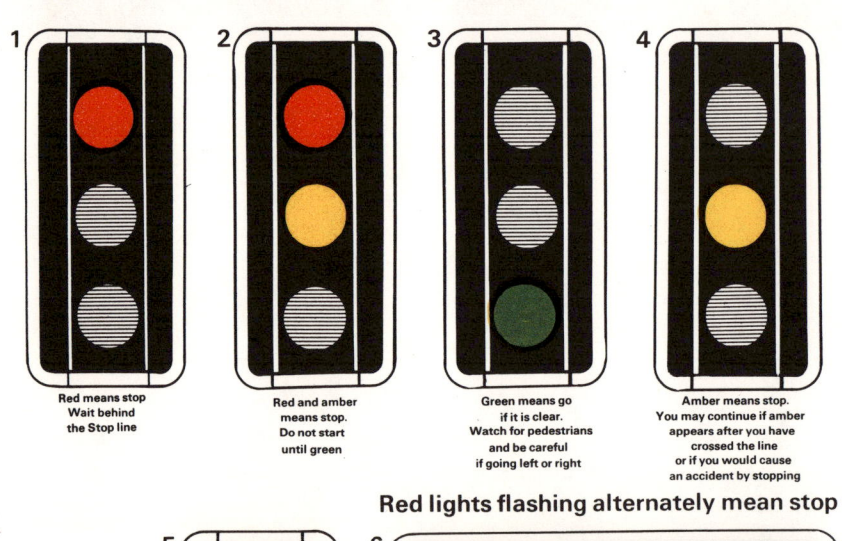

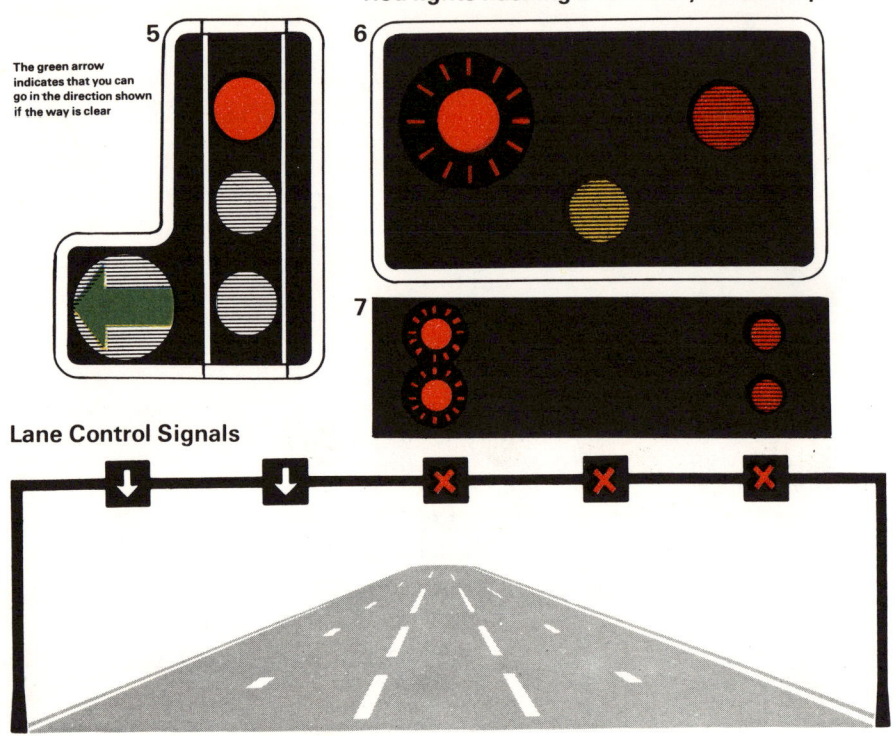

1 Red means stop. Wait behind the Stop line

2 Red and amber means stop. Do not start until green

3 Green means go if it is clear. Watch for pedestrians and be careful if going left or right

4 Amber means stop. You may continue if amber appears after you have crossed the line or if you would cause an accident by stopping

Red lights flashing alternately mean stop

5 The green arrow indicates that you can go in the direction shown if the way is clear

Lane Control Signals

White arrow – lane available to traffic facing the sign

Red cross – lane closed to traffic facing the sign

WARNING SIGNS
mostly triangular

- Cross roads
- Roundabout 
- T junction 
- Staggered junction 
- Side road 
- REDUCE SPEED NOW — Plate below some signs
- Sharp deviation of route to left (or right chevrons reversed) 
- Bend to right (or left symbol reversed)  
- GIVE WAY 50 yds — Distance to 'Give Way' line ahead 
- STOP 100 yds — Distance to 'Stop' line ahead
- Double bend first to left (may be reversed) 
- Slippery road 
- Two-way traffic straight ahead 
- Two-way traffic crosses one-way road 
- Traffic merges from left 
- Traffic merges from right 
- Road narrows on both sides 
- Dual carriageway ends 
- Steep hill downwards 
- Steep hill upwards 
- Gradients may be shown as a ratio (i.e. 20% = 1:5)
- Road works 
- Change to opposite carriageway (may be reversed) 
- Righthand lane closed (symbols may be reversed) 
- Loose chippings 
- Road narrows on right (left if symbol reversed)  
- School — Children going to or from school
- AUTOMATIC BARRIERS STOP when lights show — Plate to indicate a level crossing equipped with automatic barriers and flashing lights
- Level crossing with barriers or gate ahead 
- Level crossing without barrier or gate ahead  
- Safe height 16'-6" — Overhead electric cable plate indicates maximum height of vehicles which can pass under
- Single file traffic — Single file in each direction 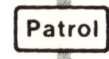
- Patrol — School crossing patrol ahead (some signs have amber lights which flash when patrol is operating)
- Hump bridge 
- Uneven road 
- Traffic signals 
- Single track road — Road wide enough for only one line of traffic 
- Ford — Worded warning sign  
- Fallen tree
- 'Count-down' markers approaching concealed level crossing (each bar represents ⅓ the distance from first warning sign to the crossing) 
- 14'-6" — Available width of headroom indicated
- Location of level crossing without barrier or gate 

59

Low flying aircraft or sudden aircraft noises  | Pedestrian Crossing  | Cattle  | Horses crossing  | Wild horses or ponies  | Wild animals

Distance to hazard (1 mile) | Distance over which hazard extends (For 2 miles) | Falling or fallen rocks  | Height limit (e.g. low bridge) 14'-6" | Quayside or river bank  | Opening bridge

Traffic Signs – signs giving orders, mostly circular

Maximum Speed (40) | National speed limit applies  | Stop and give way  | Give way to traffic on major road

School crossing patrol (STOP CHILDREN) | STOP POLICE | No entry for vehicles and traffic  | No right turn  | No left turn  | No U turns

No overtaking  | No vehicles  | No motor vehicles  | No motor vehicles except solo motorcycles, scooters or mopeds | Manually operated temporary 'Stop' sign  | No vehicle with over 12 seats except regular scheduled school and works buses

No cycling  | No pedestrians  | No goods vehicles over laden weight shown (unladen weight limit) 3 tons | No vehicles including load over weight shown (total weight limit) 10 TONS | Axle weight limit 2 TONS | No vehicles over height shown 14'-6"

No vehicles or combination of vehicles over length shown 32 feet | No vehicles over width shown 7'-6" | No stopping (clearway)  | Give priority to vehicles from opposite direction  | URBAN CLEARWAY Monday to Friday am 8-9 30 pm 4 30 6 30 — No stopping during times shown except for up to 2 min to set down or pick up passengers

Plates below some signs qualify their message

End — End of restriction | Except for loading — Except for loading/unloading goods and access to off street garaging | Except buses and coaches — Except for vehicles with over 12 seats | Except buses — Exception for stage and scheduled express carriages, school and works buses | Except for access — Exception for access to premises and land adjacent to the road where there is no alternative route

60

Signs with blue circles but no red border are mostly compulsory

- Ahead only
- Turn left ahead (right if symbol reversed) 
- Turn left (right if symbol reversed) 
- Keep left (right if symbol reversed) 
- Vehicles may pass either side to reach some destinations 
- Route to be used by pedal cyclists only 
- Minimum speed 
- End of minimum speed 
- Mini roundabout (roundabout circulation give way to vehicles from immediate right) 
- One way traffic 

With-flow bus lane

Contra-flow bus lane

Signs on primary routes green backgrounds

- ↑ Scarborough A64 / ← Pickering A169 / York A64 → — On approaches to junctions 
- A46 / Lincoln 12 / Newark 28 / (Nottingham 48) / Leicester 63 — Route confirmatory sign after junction 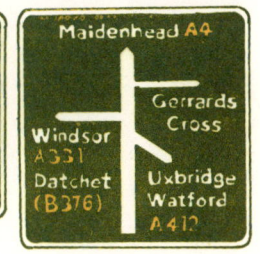
- Maidenhead A4 / Windsor A331 / Datchet (B376) / Gerrards Cross / Uxbridge / Watford A412 — On approaches to junctions 
- Sutton C'field A38 / Tamworth (A4091) → — At the junction
- (A46) Route confirmatory sign after junction 
- R Ring road

Signs on non-primary routes – black borders

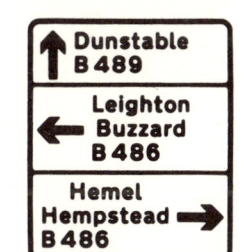

- ↑ Dunstable B489 / ← Leighton Buzzard B486 / Hemel Hempstead B486 → — On approaches to junctions
- R Ring road 
- Hemel Hempstead B486 7 → — At the junction 

Local directions signs – blue borders

- Ring road / Victoria Stn / Cringleford 2½ → — At the junction 
- ↑ Northchurch 1½ / Wiggington 4 / ← Chesham 5 / Potten End 2 / Gaddesden 3½ / Ashridge 4 ↗ — On approaches to junctions 
- Walton 4 / Stadium ½ / Race course / Cathedral ½ / Free car park / Municipal offices / Town centre / Bus station — On approaches to junctions

61

Other direction signs

(A33, M3) — Advisory route for lorries

300 yds (camping/caravan symbol) — Direction to camping or caravanning site

Wrest Park Ancient Monument — Ancient Monument

Toilets (wheelchair symbol) — Direction to toilets with access for the disabled

HR — Holiday route

Lille Barracks — Direction to Ministry of Defence establishment

Council Offices Public Library — Route for pedestrians

300 yds (picnic symbol) — Picnic site

300 yds (house symbol) — Direction to youth hostel

Gatwick 2 — Airport

INFORMATION SIGNS – all rectangular

Meter ZONE — Mon-Fri 8·30 am-6·30 pm, Saturday 8·30 am-1·30 pm — Entrance to controlled parking zone

ONE WAY — One-way street

Priority over vehicles from opposite direction

T — No through road

H Hospital — Hospital ahead

P — Parking place: plate may indicate any restrictions on use

Permit P holders only — Parking restricted to use by people named on sign

Forton Services — Direction to service areas with fuel, parking, cafeteria and restaurant facilities

Zone ENDS — End of controlled parking zone

Appropriate traffic lanes at junction ahead

'Count-down' markers at exit from motorway (each bar represents 100 yards to the exit, green backed markers may be used on primary routes)

Bus Stop — Bus stop

Bus lane — Bus lane on road at junction ahead

(bicycle symbol) — Routes available for pedal cyclists

i Tourist Information

62

ON THE MOTORWAY

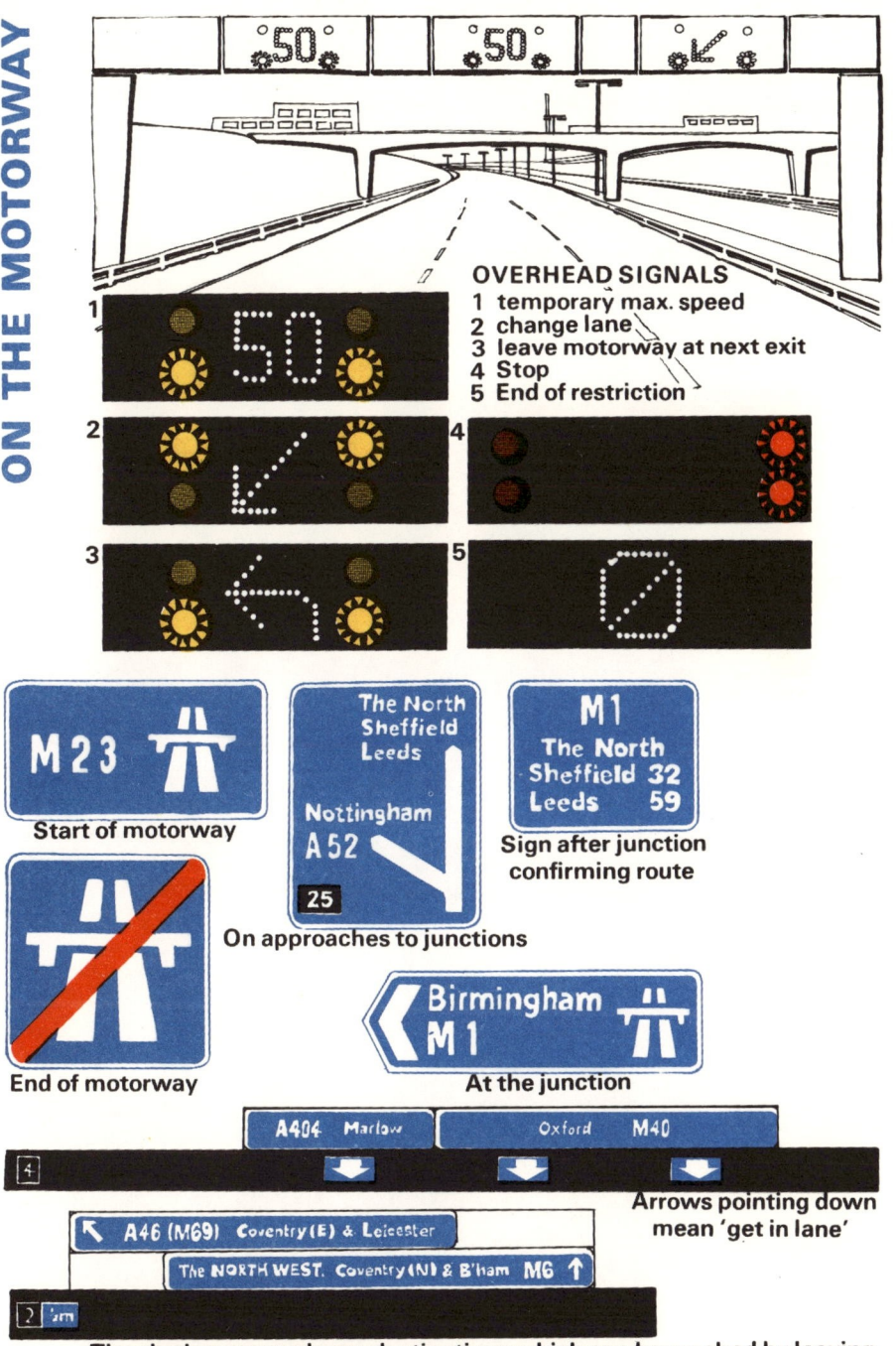

OVERHEAD SIGNALS
1 temporary max. speed
2 change lane
3 leave motorway at next exit
4 Stop
5 End of restriction

Start of motorway — M23

End of motorway

On approaches to junctions — The North, Sheffield, Leeds / Nottingham A52 / 25

Sign after junction confirming route — M1 The North, Sheffield 32, Leeds 59

At the junction — Birmingham M1

A404 Marlow | Oxford M40
Arrows pointing down mean 'get in lane'

◄ A46 (M69) Coventry (E) & Leicester
The NORTH WEST, Coventry (N) & B'ham M6 ↑

The sloping arrow shows destinations which can be reached by leaving the motorway at the next junction

63